Course in

WASH DRAWING

LEONARD BROOKS

REINHOLD PUBLISHING CORPORATION

New York

DESIGNED BY MYRON HALL, III
TYPE SET BY COMET PRESS
PRINTED BY THE GUINN COMPANY
BOUND BY RUSSELL-RUTTER

ACKNOWLEDGMENT

The author is grateful to all those who helped to make this book possible. To the artists who contributed their work for reproduction and to the many owners of pictures that have been used for illustrations herein, my many thanks.

"*In painting, it is better to be inexperienced (young in ch'i)
than stupid. It is better to be audacious than commonplace.
If the brush is hesitant, it cannot be lively; if commonplace,
it most likely will produce only banalities. If one aims to
avoid the banal, there is no other way but to study more assid-
uously both books and scrolls and so to encourage the spirit
(ch'i) to rise, for when the vulgar and the commonplace dominate
the ch'i subsides. The beginner should be hopeful and careful
to encourage it to rise.*"

*From "The Tao of Painting" by Mai-mai Sze
Reprinted through courtesy of
Bollingen Foundation, New York;
Routledge & Kegan Paul Ltd., London*

CONTENTS

FOREWORD

For many years now, sketching and painting in wash and line has been a source of delight for me, both for itself and as an aid to my work in full-color watercolor and oil painting.

It is my hope that this little book will introduce beginners and students to the joys of working within the limitations of the monochromatic medium, for there is a satisfaction in using the simple means of brush and ink that belongs to this time-honored method alone. This has been known to artists for centuries, particularly to the wise old masters of the Orient who revelled in the expressive possibilities of ink painting, and developed it to such a highly sophisticated creative level that it still surpasses our best today.

As a discipline in simplifying the complex forms of nature, the wash medium is ideal. Used as a training device in selecting and composing, it is invaluable for the student who aspires to become a skilled watercolorist or draftsman.

Within the scope of this book I have not had space to do more than cover some of the practical matters of brush and pen usage. I would like to suggest that interested readers supplement the exercises and ideas presented in the short course outlined here with a study of the books listed in the bibliography. Learning to control the brush is only part of our painting technique; learning to think and feel through our eyes as *creative artists* is another matter, one that can only be touched upon in these pages. Close study of the drawings and words of the great traditional draftsmen of the past, as well as the work of contemporary artists, may help you to find within yourself your own personal world and spirit, without which all techniques become meaningless.

San Miguel de Allende, Mexico

MATERIALS

An essential and basic outfit for wash drawing, containing everything you will need, is shown in the illustration on the opposite page. Later you may add to it or change it to suit your individual preference. With experience you will feel more at home with certain types of brushes and will like some kinds of inks and papers better than others.

The initial outlay for this equipment is reasonable. The only costly items on the list are the sable brushes. A fine large No. 14 pointed sable brush can cost twenty dollars or more, but you can manage quite well with a less expensive substitute, such as an imitation sable, or a Chinese fitch wash brush. The broad square-end brush is a lettering brush, which is obtainable in real or near-sable hair.

Fine papers are expensive, but here, too, you can use a less costly student grade, machine-made paper for your experiments. Inks and watercolors should always be of the finest quality. Cheap inks will fade and will not disperse properly; watercolors in the student grades will often vary in color and consistency from tube to tube.

Brushes and Pens

The brushes and pens illustrated are the ones I have found most useful both for sketching and studio work. Most of the drawings in this book were made with them. The Chinese brush is very useful; available in several sizes, it can be purchased in most art supply stores. The flat sable brush is useful for washes and broad detail; the small sable is for fine drawing and line work. The bamboo pen is a bamboo stick cut to pen shape. It is available in art supply stores, or can be easily made from a discarded bamboo-handled brush. One type has a reversible brush tip in one end of the pen. Turkey or goose quill pens are easy to make; with a razor blade, cut a point on a well-dried quill from which the feathers have been removed. Cut the point at an angle and trim it constantly as it wears down. An assortment of broad and fine, steel pen nibs is useful. With proper care, your brushes will give you years of good service; rinse them well after using, pull to a point and store upright in a jar. Keep pen points clean and dry to avoid rust.

Inks

There are many types of ink suitable for wash drawing. I have used standard "waterproof" inks made by Higgins, Grumbacher, Pelikan and others. Some dilute with water better than others; some are of a bluer tint, or less black; some disperse better for wet-in-wet technique. I like Chinese or Japanese inks above all. They combine well with watercolor black and wash out to a pleasing warm-toned gray. A particularly fine brand, made in Hong Kong, is called Kwong Yung (Kee Ki Co.) "Writing Ink". I have found it in most Chinese stationery stores. I have also used Japanese paste inks, which come in plastic squeeze containers, and the many varieties of "sumi" sticks—solid cakes of ink that must be ground on a stone and mixed with water. Preparing the ink in the traditional fashion is a solemn ritual in the Orient, but is a bit complicated and impractical for the out-of-doors sketcher. I find the liquid inks in bottles more practical.

Watercolor

I like ivory black better than the colder, more bluish lamp blacks. Buy the tubed pigment, not the hard cake in pans. A tube of sepia will give your ink and wash drawings an "Old Master" look, especially if you combine the washes with a quill pen technique. Another color to try is Payne's gray, a cold blue-black which combines well with tinted papers. For variety, add one or two other colors to your equipment, and experiment with them. It is surprising how full-color can be suggested with only one or two pigments.

Papers

An entire book could be devoted to this subject. On page 33 I have shown a few of the many papers used for wash drawing and watercolor work. There are vast differences in the qualities and surface characteristics of artists' papers. The more types you use, the sooner you will be able to determine your preferences.

Have no doubt that the expensive papers really are the best papers, both for working on and for their non-fading permanence. Cheap papers are made from wood pulp or rehashed scrap, with sizing, bleaches, waxes and fillers added to give body and surface smoothness. Fine papers are generally hand-made, often from clean rags or linen, their textures and surfaces beautifully contrived for the transparent washes of the painter. Student-grade papers are reasonably priced and are ideal for practice, but there is nothing like a fine sheet of paper to inspire good work. Splurge occasionally on Whatman, Fabriano, D'Arches, Strathmore and American Watercolor Society papers; their inviting textures will propel you to work. I like 140 to 300 pound sheets for large sketches. The papers are dampened and stretched on a drawing board to prevent buckling. Use gummed paper tape and thumbtacks, and the watercolor paper will dry out as tight as a drum.

Chinese and Japanese papers have magnificent surfaces but are most difficult to work with; they are fragile, often absorbent, and require a sure and delicate touch. Rice papers are available in a variety of thicknesses, ranging from butterfly-wing weight to medium weight.

Other Useful Equipment
Water jar
Paint rags, paper tissues,
 a small sponge
Eraser, razor blade
Conté crayons, soft pencils,
 charcoal sticks
Wax crayons, white
Rubber cement or frisket liquid
Mixing slab or paint box
Masking tape
Sketching stool
Fishing-tackle box or knapsack
Drawing board and spring clips
Portfolio, sketch book
Fixative with atomizer, or in spray can

SABLES

BAMBOO

WRITING PENS (ASSORTED)

CHINESE BRUSH →

TURKEY QUILL

BRUSHES AND PENS

WATER JAR

PAINT-BOX

ERASER

PAINT RAG

SPONGE

INK

BLACK CHINESE OR INDIA INK

RAZOR BLADES

SEPIA AND BLACK WATERCOLOR

PUT A LINE AROUND IT!

If you are interested enough to want to read this book, it is reasonable to assume that you have had some training or experience with the mechanics of drawing. This does not imply professional facility and ease of execution but means that you have probably spent some time in the pursuit of drawing—learning how to control the eye and hand so that they work together in putting down lines and masses on paper.

If you are a beginner who self-consciously ties himself into knots when faced with the representation of objects, live or inanimate, perhaps a few words on this subject are in order. First of all, before you begin to draw, relax. Forget about all the things you have heard or read regarding perspective, foreshortening, proportion,

blocking-out, shading. Some of these will be helpful later; but for the beginner they are often a hindrance and an inhibiting factor. More likely than not, you are interested in drawing because it is pleasurable and enjoyable. Don't make it a chore. Training the eye to see and the hand to respond will take time, but it can be fun.

Take a pen with a thick nib, or a small, pointed sable brush. Dip it in black ink. Look around you and pick out some object; choose a simple form, such as a jug, an apple, an ash-tray, or a lamp. Study it carefully; assess its shape; stamp it into your mind; *really* look at it. Now face up to your paper and *put a line around it!* Work swiftly, using as continuous a line as possible. Don't be concerned if your drawing appears out of proportion, crooked, top-heavy. With practice it will become much easier. Use no timid sketching-in with pencil first. Sit well back from your work and move your wrist freely. Draw large, rather than small, tight, cramped. Do several line drawings of the same object, analyzing the object repeatedly before beginning each drawing. Does it fit into a ball? A cube? A rectangle? Is it a combination of several basic solid forms? Sort out these questions in your mind before you draw.

If you make a habit of doing this exercise, covering a number of pages with objects like those shown here, you will soon develop confidence in your drawing ability. More complicated subjects will follow and before long you will be able to combine more difficult forms, including the figure.

Try the "scribble" free line, too, drawing *around and through* the object. This is in contrast with silhouette drawing, and takes the line on an adventuresome journey, assessing the solidity of a form, and suggesting it on the flatness of the paper.

The free line drawing above was made with a bamboo pen and Chinese ink. Contour drawings of complicated forms like these peach branches become easier to do if you train your eye first by drawing simple silhouettes of less complex subjects, such as those shown on the preceding page.

At right is a sketchbook note made with touches of gray wash over a loose pen drawing jotted down while enjoying a "refresco" at an open-air table in the plaza, Oaxaca, Mexico.

BLACK, WHITE AND GRAY

Here are the fundamental elements of wash drawing with which we will work—blacks, intermediate grays and white. These are the notes with which we will compose our music. If you study the illustrations carefully, you will reach some basic understanding of painting in black and white wash. Translating the varied colors and infinite forms of nature into manageable tonal schemes is the problem before us. The subtle nuances of grays, the interplay of white areas against blacks—these require practice and control. Techniques, the appreciation and instinct for good design, the skills necessary for achieving visual interest by contrast, repetition, animation of static surfaces are all developed through these simple exercises. Take a page and make variations of your own based on these easy demonstrations.

Above are two tones of gray, a medium gray and a near-black. Learn to make comparisons of relative darkness; place these tones in the scale of grays you make by adding water to black ink. Think of these tones of grays as steps. Train your eye to make any desired tonal value at will.

At left is a gradated scale made without separations between the steps. Begin with water at the top of the scale and gradually add pigment; or begin with the darks first and add water, brushing evenly from side to side without scrubbing.

The stairway at right is made from separated tones ranging from dark to light.

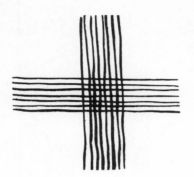

Consider the straight line and its visual interest. Repeat it or cross it and see how this interest increases. Try a series of the same length, using a heavier stroke. Cross-hatch two sets of parallels.

Add the enrichment of a few free forms of tone to your linear pattern and you will create design interest of a simple kind. The white surface gains variety of a primitive order. Next, try the same combination of design elements, using curved lines and brush strokes as shown at left, below. Try a note of gray over flowing strokes of leaf forms, similar to those below at right. Notice how the eye is pleased by the addition of the gray tone against the stark black and white contrast.

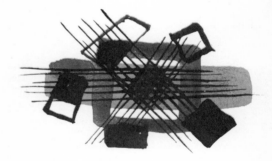

Now review the steps above with a simple exercise. Cover an entire page with conventions of this kind, using objects or merely lines, dots and tonal areas.

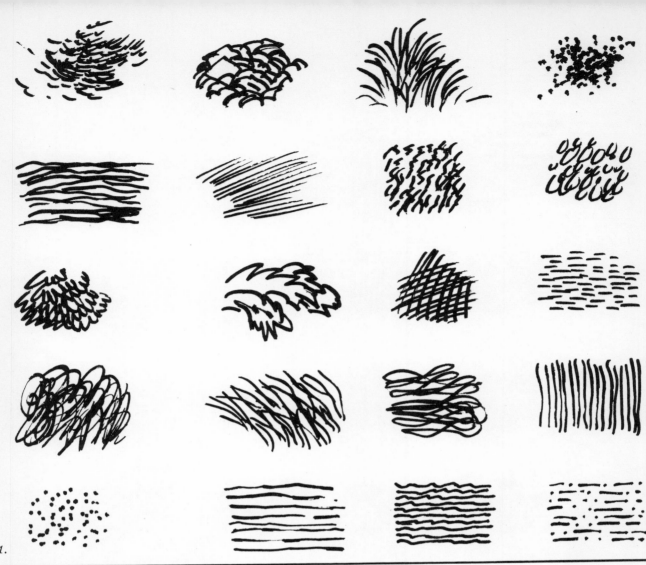

1.

2.

14

TEXTURES

1. *Pen textures can be used to enrich underlying washes in combined pen and wash drawings. At left is a chart of sixteen pen textures composed of simple lines, dots and dashes. Make a chart of your own pen textures, using these simple elements.*

2. *A wash is applied over textures in varying degrees of light and dark tone values taken from the gray scale.*

3. *Textures of pen lines and brush strokes are combined with numerous wash tones assembled haphazardly. Straight and curved lines are juxtaposed, contrasted, overlaid. A pattern emerges, but it is too busy with textured agitations. While it might be pleasing for an all-over print, with the pattern repeated many times, it is tiresome as a single unit.*

3.

4. *Emphasis and controlled selection begin to appear. The same notes, textures and shapes are rearranged into a more satisfying order. One large white area (a door indication turns it into a house) anchors the other shapes. A black accent dominates the foreground, contrasting with the white area. Curved and straight lines play about these two spots, echoing and repeating the smaller black and white areas. The same elements have been used as in drawing No. 3, but a constructed design emerges.*

4.

5. *Repetition, rhythms, and the necessary design elements are everywhere about us, becoming visible when we begin to understand what to look for and what to select. See how effectively they are utilized in this simple rendering of trees on a hilltop.* We must learn to distill what we need from what we see, and leave the rest.

5.

SPOT OUT THE BLACKS

The black accent! What would the artist do without it? This is the affirmative note, as definite and insistent as a drumbeat. Learn to make it work for you; muffle it in grays, or let it emerge loudly when contrasted against whites. Use it as a strong, sharp silhouette, or spot it out where you need to pin-point the interest.

For the beginner, the discipline of using black accents is excellent training for composing in line and mass. Lean on the side of simplicity, always. It is surprising how often a sketch can be pulled together by the strategic placement of a dark mass as an anchor on which the entire composition rides. Lead the eye to it; spot it out in an important area of your picture and let the rest of the composition work around it. Be sure that the blacks work for you; they will give punch to your drawings and vitality to your quick figure sketches and rapid studies.

MAKE THE WHITES COUNT

ROBERT MAXWELL

This portrait sketch is a fine example of a drawing in which the white areas of paper are used to good advantage. Notice how the features have been brushed in suggestively, without excessive detail.

Just as the spotting of the blacks is important to the sketch, so is the planning of the white spaces and areas. The professional artist knows how to use the white paper as a foil for the other tones, preserving it where possible, covering it only after much thought, for once gone, it is gone irrevocably and no amount of patching, touching-up with white paint, or scraping will bring back the sparkle of the original surface. An occasional razor-blade scratch, a touch of sandpaper to remove a spot, or pre-planned masking are legitimate aids, not patch-up devices.

Surround a white area with black and see how this area looks lighter to the eye than the rest of the paper around it. Sometimes the white will look *too* white by contrast and must be toned to hold its place, or it will appear to jump out from the surrounding black. Make the test by placing several light and medium gray tones in a black matrix.

BAMBOO AND BRUSH

As early as the fifth century, Chinese artists were striving to follow the teachings of their master, Hsieh Ho, who spoke of such things as the essential quality of brush drawing as "rhythmic vitality and life movement." How to bring the brush strokes to life, how to imprison in them the intense feelings and emotions of man before nature, how to express the inner essence of an object—these were the concerns of the painters.

Recently in the United States there has been a renewed awareness of the great oriental traditions, arts and philosophies. Although you may not have the urge to undertake an investigation of the spiritual teachings of Zen or the involved traditions of the *Tao* of painting, as a student of art you will find that there is a great deal of fascinating and valuable material worth studying in the drawings and paintings of the earlier oriental artists.

There are a number of books on the subject now available in inexpensive paper-bound editions; several are listed in the bibliography. In them you will find the absorbing story of the formal interpretation of the "Four Gentlemen" —the bamboo, plum, orchid and chrysanthemum —by generations of artist-poets, and the precise and wonderful descriptions of the "Eight Laws of Ledges for Painting Mountains, Rocks, and Cliffs," and other strangely didactic rules.

Much of our contemporary painting has an obvious relationship to the techniques of the oriental artist. The bold stroke of the "action painter," the calligraphy-like brush work, the symbols of many of our painters echo the free sweeping stroke that Chinese and Japanese masters cultivated and perfected. The artist is concerned today, more than ever, with the spontaneity and "life-flow" of his conception, rather than the rigid recording of the cold, visual fact. Perhaps this explains why the contemporary artist finds much that is close to his personal vision in the works of the painters of the ancient

The brush strokes depicting bamboo, reproduced in actual size above and at lower left, were done with a Japanese pointed brush in black ink on rice paper. You can see how an effort was made to give the single brush-stroke shading—the sui-boku quality, which means ink and water shaded in blacks and grays in one brush stroke.

Orient. The student of art history will find it interesting to note the present revival of the oriental influence, which so profoundly affected the work of many men who painted at the close of the nineteenth century—Whistler, Van Gogh, Bonnard, and many others.

Many of the technical devices of the oriental artist have been absorbed and adapted to western methods of painting. In the media of wash drawing and full watercolor, the contemporary artist has learned how to exploit the wet brush-stroke in a transparent, free manner on various paper surfaces. Instead of the raw silks of the Orient, textured papers of brilliant white were used, and gradually the distinctive wash quality, freshly and cleanly stated, became the criterion for a fine piece of work. Unfortunately, this transparent, loose brush technique became an ob-

session; as a result, content and significance of statement was lost in the effort to make "nice clean washes." A reaction followed, and for a few years many watercolor societies showed nothing but "mixed techniques"—everything but the traditionally clean, fresh watercolor. Today the intelligent student makes use of all forms of wash—transparent, mixed, or combined techniques.

This reproduction of "Autumn Woods" is an example of the fusion of oriental and traditional approaches. The symbols of trees were scratched out; the wet, direct brush-strokes of foliage were treated in a decorative manner reminiscent of the oriental style. Yet the flavor of the English watercolor school was retained.

BRUSH CONTROL

The brush is the most important tool in your wash drawing outfit; pens, quills and bamboo sticks are auxiliaries to it. The three types of brushes illustrated on page 9 are to the artist what the bow is to the violinist. Learn to control the brush so that you can use it as delicately or strongly as you wish, just as the violinist varies the pressure on the bow. Use fast and slow strokes to vary the tempo of the marks you make on paper. Each brush has its own characteristics; you will learn how the square brush obtains textures different from those made by the pointed one; how the stroke widens when painted downward, and pulls to a point when brushed upward. You must learn the peculiarities of sable and fitch brushes, how each holds water and ink for wash-making. A thorough knowledge of the scope and the limitations of your brushes is the "secret" that will help you to master the art of wash drawing.

The dispersions and granulations of ink on wet paper are exploited in the "wet-in-wet" technique. Try varying degrees of wetness, from a semi-dry sponged paper from which the surplus water has been removed, to the well-soaked, very wet paper which must remain flat on a table. Float and drop ink onto the paper with a brush; experiment with different pen lines. With practice you will know what kind of line will remain after the paper dries. Touch in details while the paper is still partially wet, or after it has dried completely, for a variety of soft and hard linear effects.

Here are a number of exercises for practice. Make up your own pages of controlled and free strokes. Use the wrist as well as the fingers. Try painting standing up at a desk, or at an easel with your work at a slant. The more pages you cover with such experimental strokes the sooner you will be able to control the brush and achieve the strokes you need whenever you need them.

The original of the sketch above, "Jungle Edge," was drawn with yellow and black inks, resulting in a very effective quality of diffused lights filtering down through the trees. The painting was done on very wet paper in order to keep all edges blurred and soft. Notice the economy of detail, the shadowy wash areas in the center of the composition, suggestive of the impenetrable depth of the jungle growth.

Outlines of the bulbous shapes of the cactus plant at right were drawn on wet paper to give an appropriate softness to the rounded forms. The spiny cactus needles, sharp and hard, provide interesting textural contrast. See how the black accents add unity to the simple composition.

LINE AND WASH

The photograph shows a rugged stretch of Nova Scotia shore which was used as the subject for the two studies reproduced on these pages. The sketch on the opposite page is a line drawing made with two pens. One pen produced a fine, thin line; the heavy, broad line was made with a bamboo stick, but could also have been produced with a turkey quill. This combination of fine and heavy lines is an effective method for achieving variety and interest in your drawings, and also serves to emphasize depth and perspective. The heavy lines used in the foreground point up the nearness of the rocks on the beach, while the use of fine lines for drawing the fish shed, water and boats helps these more distant objects to recede visually, keeps them in place in the background.

The same variations in thickness of line shown in the line drawing were used in the wash drawing of the same subject, shown below. The paper was first dampened with a sponge; then the thin lines were drawn in. The need for speedy drawing is evident here; to achieve the soft, blurred effect characteristic of this technique, the ink must disperse and run *before* the paper dries. The rocks, stones and moss on the beach in the foreground were suggested with the wet-in-wet technique described in detail in the section immediately preceding these pages. When the drawing was completely dry, a few hard black line accents were added to define the forms. Textures on the large boulders were achieved with dry-brush, augmenting the wet-on-wet; white highlights in the darker wash areas were etched in with a few scratches of a razor blade.

23

DRY BRUSH

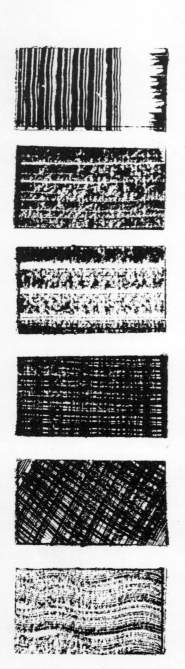

A valuable adjunct to tone building with flat washes is shown here. The dry brush effect is obtained by rubbing out most of the ink or water-color from the brush onto a scrap of paper before painting. Pointed or square-ended, or even old and worn bristle brushes can be utilized for making dry brush textures. A wide range of

In "The Maria Elena," below, the dry brush was useful to give textural variety to the edges of the overhanging palm fronds at the top of the picture. The dry brush strokes were applied while the surface of the paper was partially wet. In the foreground a spatter technique was used to suggest the litter on the beach. In this technique, the paint from a well-loaded brush is "flicked" onto the picture. Make sure there are no bystanders nearby when "flicking"!

The detail of palm fronds at right, reproduced in actual size, illustrates the manner in which the brush stroke "breaks" on the surface of the paper.

dabbed and stippled surfaces can be evolved, as well as many types of strokes that produce numerous lines with one stroke of the brush.

Develop textures by crossing over lines, combining stipple and line, employing several different brushes. Try an assortment of papers ranging from smooth to rough; each paper will provide a different effect. Use the same dry brush strokes first on dry paper and then on damp paper, and note the variation which can be achieved. Use waterproof inks for your dry brush work if you plan to paint washes over it; use the dry brush over washes when areas need enlivening.

MASKING

Although considered by some purists of wash drawing to be a trick, the device of masking can be used to good purpose if done with care. Masking must be planned ahead of time in order to preserve the virgin whiteness of the paper. Special masking tape is used for this technique; similar to adhesive tape, it has the advantage of being made with an adhesive material that will not tear or otherwise alter the surface of the paper when removed. Strips or spots of masking tape are affixed to the paper in pre-planned areas, forming a protective mask when the wash or ink is applied. Then the tape is peeled off, leaving the paper exposed. After the tape has been removed, accents can be touched in, or the whites can be modelled, as in the accents on the slender birch trees in the study below, made with the masking technique.

PEEL TAPE OFF   STRIPS OF TAPE

WASHES OVER TAPE

Before washes are applied, a white paraffin candle or white wax crayon can be used to obtain interesting broken white surfaces, as in the studies above and at right. After the wash dries, the paper can also be scraped down with a razor blade to bring up the white even lighter if desired. Some papers absorb the wax more readily than others; experiment is needed to find the paper most suited to the use of this technique.

Rubber cement, too, may be used for masking, since it will reject washes subsequently applied. Use a stick or an old brush for rubber cement masking; don't use a good brush, or it will be ruined. The rubber cement is rubbed off with the finger or a soft eraser when the wash is dry; fascinating patterns can be created with this technique. A liquid frisket material commonly used by commercial artists is available in art supply stores. Similar to rubber cement in its masking qualities, it is thinner, and may be painted on with a brush for masking in finer detail.

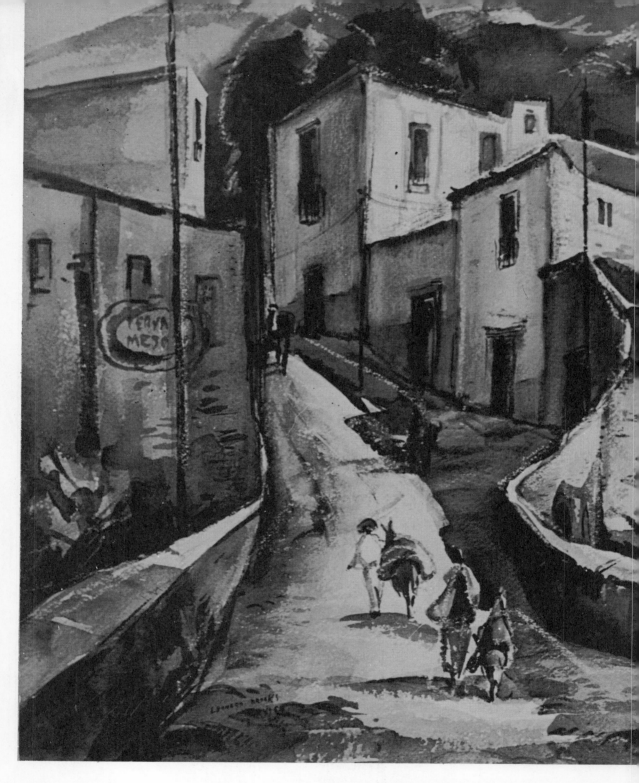

COMBINED TECHNIQUES

1. In the sketch at the top of the opposite page, dry brush strokes have been employed to give texture and solidity to the buildings. See how the same type of dry brush stroke has been used in the large painting above, giving sparkle and surface interest to the walls and road.

1.

2.

3.

2. In this sketch, a razor blade was used to flatten out the wash while still wet, creating a new texture.

3. Before the washes were applied, white crayon was used in the bottom sketch at right. The ink washes were rejected by the waxed surfaces of the paper, leaving white areas to suggest the figures. Crayon lines can also be seen in the mountains and on the road in the large painting at left.

SKETCHBOOKS

Develop the sketchbook habit so that it becomes second nature for you to jot down ideas and sketches for later reference. Put down written reminders which will help you to recall the moment and mood of the day, the direction of the sun, the length of the shadows, the force of the wind, the construction of buildings. Pertinent information of this kind will be invaluable to you later, when you develop the sketch into a more finished state in the studio.

Wash drawings can often be made on location when the day does not lend itself to painting in color. At high noon, for example, the light is often bleached, dull and unsuitable for color work. On the other hand, this kind of daylight may be ideal for transposing a subject into tones of black and white. The sketch at the top of the facing page was made on Nantucket Island at mid-day, with the sun directly overhead. A felt-nib pen was used to establish the drawing. Over this the washes were applied with sepia water-color; the dark tones were kept in sharp contrast with the white paper to achieve the effect of intense, brilliant sunlight.

As you gain experience in the use of tonal washes, you will turn the surprises and vagaries of nature to good advantage. Some strange and wonderful evening, a stretch of landscape which you may have passed a hundred times will suddenly catch a gleam of light or be bathed in a haze of silver mist. The subject becomes alive and irresistible. This is the time for a quick notation, even a few lines and dabs of tone, to help you capture a synthesis which can be worked on and embellished at a later, more appropriate time. Try to put down the essence of the moment; search out the lines, forms and tones which, when united, evoke the magic moment that attracted your attention. Look for the large, strong forms. They are probably the backbone of the composition's lure. Note the way the shadows fall, how they set the planes of the landscape in relief and define space against space. Keep the light consistent; notice how the direction of the sunlight slants all the shadows to one side. Consider the details and evaluate their contribution to the whole; determine how they can be indicated without detracting from the over-all effect that first aroused your interest.

Your ability to recall these sensations for later use will increase rapidly if you discipline your eye and your mind with problems designed to train your memory. Stop before a composition you have always intended to paint. Study it meticulously, without putting down a single line on paper; but draw the lines and tones on an imaginary mental page to stamp it firmly in your memory. Then go back to your studio, or face away from the scene, and try to record the essential movement of the composition's lines and forms. Endeavor to record the feeling of the place, rather than the literal accuracy of detail. Exercises of this kind will help you to sharpen your memory, as well as teach you how to distill the essential structure of a composition from the clutter of detail which may surround and obscure it.

Strong shadows created by side-lighting will help establish the planes of the landscape. See how they give depth and dimension to the walls in the foreground and the mountains in the background, in the sketch at right. Tones have been limited to one medium gray plus white, with black brush outlines used to define the drawing.

CHARCOAL | FELT PEN | PENCIL | PEN AND INK | BAMBOO PEN | WAX CRAYON | BROWN

SEVEN SKETCHING TECHNIQUES

Making a panel like the one above, but from a subject of your own choosing, will be a valuable experiment in the use of assorted media. This panel, shown at greatly reduced size, was made on a strip cut from a full sheet of watercolor paper of medium rough texture. Such a texture is suitable for a wide range of lines, from fine pen to charcoal.

If *charcoal* is used as a sketching medium, preparatory to making a wash drawing, be sure to dust off the excess charcoal or spray the sketch with a light coat of fixative; use a fixative that will not repel the washes. A plastic spray is unsuitable for this purpose, since it will not permit the washes to penetrate; a light shellac-alcohol fixative is recommended, as it will not seal the paper surface to later washes if applied with care. Charcoal can also be used over wash drawings, and then sprayed with a fixative.

The *felt-pen* technique is quite effective for rapid sketching and note-taking. The drawing at the top of page 31 illustrates the kind of lines the felt pen can produce. It is a rather risky medium for permanent work, fading badly when framed and exposed to sunlight. I use it primarily for sketchbook work, where the paper is not exposed to light, but is stored away for reference purposes only. Washes sit well over the felt-pen inks which are available in an assortment of colors as well as browns and purple-blacks.

Pencil drawing is a natural base for the use of wash. It is important not to use too soft a pencil unless you fix your sketch before applying the wash, since the lead particles will sully the wash and gray it down a tone or more. I prefer a medium dark or HB pencil for sketching prior to applying wash or watercolor.

Inks vary greatly. I have found Higgins waterproof ink most satisfactory for producing a rich black which will not run when washed over. Experiment with an assortment of pen nibs, from the most flexible to the stiffest points of writing pens, in all thicknesses. One or two will appeal to you more than others. There is a specially-designed sketching fountain pen now on the market which holds India ink without clogging—a very handy addition to your sketching outfit, particularly useful for making quick sketches and notes when traveling.

Bamboo pens have been mentioned previously. Lacking bamboo, you can try ordinary sharpened wooden sticks. An interesting broken line can be made with them. One well-known Mexican artist likes to draw with ink and matchsticks.

White wax crayons or ordinary paraffin candles will introduce a new note to your work, providing textures which can be washed over or scratched into. Press hard on the crayon to wax the paper sufficiently to repel the wet washes.

Sepia and brown inks are pleasant to work with. They can produce most effective results when used alone, or when combined with water to make lighter tones. Experiment with a combination of brown and black inks to develop your own rich brown color. These inks are particularly effective on tinted papers.

PAPERS

The segmented sketch on this page is composed of six different papers. The same tones of wash were brushed over all the papers at one time, resulting in an interesting range of effects. In WATERCOLOR—A CHALLENGE I illustrated how even color itself will change from one paper to another, due to differences in absorbency and sizing, and the nature of the processes and materials used in manufacture.

When you try a paper for the first time, make notes on its particular characteristics. How does the wash settle on the paper? Does it penetrate, or float on the surface? Does its texture take the brush strokes smoothly, or do they break in dry-brush fashion? Evaluate a paper's whiteness in comparison with other papers. It is surprising how white a paper may appear, until it is placed alongside papers of a brighter white. Contrast a hand-made Whatman with most other papers; the others will look creamy and dull in relation to the Whatman.

Try many weights and surfaces, from the smooth illustration papers and boards to the roughest granulated papers, which need scrub-bing into to get the wash on the paper. Some papers provide more satisfactory results if they are first stretched, then washed with clean water and allowed to dry before use. I have found this to be the case with some Fabriano papers which seem to have a size somewhat repellent to the first wash. Some papers hold the inks and pigments well when wet, but bleach out after drying, so that the tones appear to fade. Other papers cause black washes to dry with a hard edge. All of these peculiarities will be revealed to you when you make your own comparative panel, patterned after the one shown here.

Notice the inclusion of David Cox paper, a straw-colored paper with an attractive texture. Tinted charcoal papers are light-weight inexpensive papers made by Ingres and Michelet which will take washes nicely if not overworked, scratched with razor blades, or scrubbed. Try them for spot sketching where direct notation and summing-up demands direct painting. (See the color illustrations on pages 38 and 39 for examples of the use of some of these papers in combination with one and two colored inks.)

ATHMORE STRATION | GRUMBACHER AQUARELLE | WHATMAN SEMI-ROUGH | D'ARCHES ROUGH | DAVID COX | TINTED CHARCOAL PAPER

OUT-OF-DOORS

Weather Moods

Rain, snow, driving wind and bending trees, the fluent brush of the wash artist delights in such displays of the elements. Here is your chance to use the rich wet-in-wet washes, the strong tonal contrasts, and the powerful lines expressive of the forces rampant.

Very often such sketches must be developed from memory in the studio, sheltered from blasting winds and falling rain drops. Close observation and quick notations are in order; they will enable you to recapture the exciting moment on paper, later.

The development of a landscape "sense" will take time. Drawing trees that "feel" like trees requires much study and experience. How do you suggest millions of leaves with a few pen scrawls or the dab of a brush-stroke? What convention will you adopt for representing branches of foliage? How do we make meaningful the dots and dashes at our disposal?

Study the master drawings of Guardi, the work of men like Turner and Delacroix, to discover the variations possible in the classical tradition. The stylizations of oriental masters such as Hokusai and Hiroshige are well worth the investment of time spent for inspection and careful analysis.

"Lake and Sky," reproduced at right, was drawn on an 8" x 10" watercolor pad directly from the subject. Some paper areas were dampened, and a razor blade was discreetly used over them to flatten out the planes of the water in the foreground.

The drawing below, "Wind in the Trees," was done out of doors on a day when strong gusts blew the boughs in dancing, moving rhythms. The excitement of these forms in motion demanded bold handling, with blobs of ink and thin lines worked rapidly on thick, semi-damp paper. The drawing was recorded quickly to catch the spirit and intensity of the setting.

"Rainy Landscape" at left, depicting an impending cloudburst moving across the landscape, was made from a small pencil-scribble recorded on the back of an envelope. A moment after the sketch was completed, the entire landscape was obliterated by a gray sheet of rain. The mood of the moment was captured in the rich darks, heavy watercolor black dropped onto soaked paper, and a few lights in fence posts and foreground grass picked out with a razor blade while the paint was still wet.

PANORAMAS

Drawing a panoramic subject is always difficult: how much to include? how much to leave out? The effect achieved is dependent upon meticulous, precise planning of every element in the drawing.

The two sketches on this page are vignetted, that is, the corners and sides of the sketch have been allowed to fade out without detail, the white paper alone suggesting space. In painting a pan-oramic subject, you must try to grasp the signifi-cant forms underlying the detail. Simplify the trees to large masses, the mountains to two or three large areas of light and dark, to indicate the solidity of the formation. The use of the dark ac-cent is most evident in the sketch of the tropical village where accents and details are placed a-gainst a broad, one-wash mountain form.

COMMENTS ON WASH PAINTINGS IN COLOR

Effective variety may be added to your wash drawings by the use of tinted papers or the combining of two or more colored inks or watercolors. Shown in color on pages 38 and 39 are some examples which may suggest new combinations for experiment.

1. Painted entirely with one tone, Payne's gray on an olive tinted Ingres charcoal paper, 19 x 24 inches. A large flat sable and one pointed "rigger" brush was used; the sketch was made while sitting in a car.

2. Another rapid note made on Chinese rice paper using an ink mixed from a black Chinese ink and some brown Higgins waterproof ink. A few washes of yellow ochre plus the many tones from the ink gives a feeling of many more colors than were actually used. Painted with one large flat sable and a bamboo pen for linear detail.

3. Yellow ochre, alizarin crimson, ultramarine, Payne's gray. Four colors were used here to paint a full sketch from the subject. Wash drawing technique develops here into the full-blown watercolor. Painted on a stretched sheet of Strathmore white charcoal paper in one sitting and not touched later in the studio. Size 17 x 21 inches.

4. A flower study done with lamp-black washes and a tint of red ink for contrast. Painted freely with a sable brush using some dry brush work on a peach colored surface. Try other combinations of two tones.

5. Try combining two inks, using them separately on the sketch. Here the washes of foliage, shadows, etc. were painted with sepia-brown ink. The bark textures and other lines were drawn in with black undiluted ink over the washes. A warm tinted Ingres paper was used.

1. MARKET PLACE

2. STREET SCENE

3. MOUNTAIN VILLAGE

4. FLOWER STUDY

5. TREES

STREETS AND WALLS

The drawing of architectural subjects requires some knowledge of perspective and up- and down-hill indication, along with the ability to select and compose. Houses and streets can be rendered in dull, factual style, or they can be represented in a lively manner which carries them beyond the level of literal, photographic drawing.

As with all wash drawing, the representation of architectural subjects depends on light and dark patterns, textures, and, of primary importance, the manner in which essential elements are emphasized and organized, omitting superfluous details which might weaken the composition. Selecting a point of view and then capitalizing upon it may seem like an easy recipe for a good sketch, but to do it well requires constant practice. Here are some hints to help you on your next sketching safari.

Choose a comfortable spot if possible, sheltered from the sun and wind. A parked car can be a secluded, weather-protected studio.

Determine the proportion most suitable for the subject you plan to sketch. Do not always work in the same proportion; try long horizontals, exaggerated verticals, rectangles that are almost squares.

Draw in the major structural lines first, leaving details for later work. Work all over your sketch from the moment you begin, not in just one area at a time.

Sepia ink on toned paper was used for the down-hill exercise reproduced above. All washes were drawn first with a large broad brush. Over these the bamboo pen was used to strengthen the construction of buildings with firm lines, and to indicate foliage on the trees.

Establish an eye-level, and observe the way the lines in your composition run up or down to it.

Keep in mind that you are creating a drawing, not taking a photograph. Take as many liberties as you like, but only when you have good reason. Don't turn things upside-down or inside-out merely to be different or to make your drawings look "modern." Such distortions are just cheating, and won't work.

In the architectural study below, loose washes of lamp-black watercolor on wet paper were used first. Over these a smaller brush was employed for drawing in the detail. White paper was carefully preserved for contrast with the rich blacks.

In the down-hill study above, drawn on Ingres
charcoal paper, notice how all the lines of win-
dows, doors and roofs go upward to meet at the
point where the eye-level would be. Such subjects
are fun to do once you have mastered the basic
tenets of perspective drawing.

SEVEN WASH DRAWINGS ANALYZED

The photograph above was taken after the two sketches shown here were made during a sketching trip to Quebec. Both studies were made in a morning's work. It is interesting to compare the scene recorded by the camera with the sketches of the same setting viewed through the artist's eye. Many details of wires, television antennae and poles have been omitted in the sketch, at left, and in the wash drawing on the opposite page. Notice, too, how the camera eye flattens out the far mountains; in the wash drawing they have been made more prominent, improving the composition.

Quebec Village

The photograph and sketches on these two pages depict a spring scene on the St. Lawrence River in Quebec. The trees are still bare, and the strong shapes of far-off mountains stretch into the distance beyond the dark forms of farm houses.

First a trial sketch was made in lampblack watercolor to establish the composition. Such a sketch need not take long; it can be done on a small scale in a matter of minutes. Intruding wires and poles, which did not add to the composition, were automatically eliminated. It is always a shock to me to see a photograph of a place I have painted. The camera includes so much that has no value for the painter. In this instance I was amazed to see how many annoying details cluttered the scene. I literally did not see them as I painted. With training, the artist sees only what he wants to see, concentrating on the large theme essential to his drawing.

My first rapid sketch did not catch the flavor of the subject, but it did help me to decide what to include and what to omit. A new composition was sketched with a few light pencil lines; the transparent washes of grays were built up over the drawing, painted with a broad, flat brush into the sponged paper. First the sky, mountains and middle distance were indicated. Then a rich dark was used to delineate the house. This established the tonal range to be used, from the lightest paper areas to the darkest darks of the painting.

The first few minutes of sketching are most important. I like to put some large areas on the white surface, to destroy the empty space and let the picture get off to a good start. Work all over the page, not in one section; keep the picture moving. Try to keep your original concept constantly in mind; do not be seduced by details or carried away by changing lights or new cloud formations which are bound to occur during the painting session.

Along the Shore

The wash study of the boats, shown above, was made in the strong light of afternoon when the contrasts of light and dark lend themselves best to sketching. The gray tones of the sky act as a foil for the light areas of the boat hull. The discarded nets and debris in the foreground provide ample opportunity for all the texture-making the brush can manage. In a subject such as this, the character of the abandoned boats, the broken masts and tattered ropes are noted carefully and drawn precisely. This is a frank and realistic rendering of a romantic subject, and its detail is part of the story. It *is* composed and planned, but the structural design is secondary, and the literal interpretation of the scene is emphasized. Such subjects are well-worn themes, but they are not easy to paint. They demand drawing ability, keen observation and a knowledge of boats and the sea. This may not add up to sophisticated art, but such themes do provide excellent subject matter for sketching.

The wash and pen drawing shown opposite is another seashore sketch. Its composition is more unified, with greater attention devoted to designing the surface of the paper, breaking up the space, and relating the movement of light and dark areas within the picture plane. The linear structure of the composition is stressed, rather than concealed. The difference in the two approaches is quite evident when the sketches are compared. Which approach provides more visual satisfaction?

Oddly enough, there is not much distortion or altering of fact in the pen and wash drawing. To the native boy looking over my shoulder as I worked, I seemed to be drawing only what I saw before me, in quite a truthful and reportorial fashion. Actually, much of the subject matter was altered in a subtle way; a house was shifted there, a space left here; the sand and logs in the foreground were patterned by selection, accent and emphasis. Essentials were brought into strong relief, and minor parts of the composition were underplayed.

The study at left is a direct and rather literal brush and wash drawing made on the spot, on a full sheet of watercolor paper. The preliminary sketching was done lightly in pencil; washes were then applied.

Pen and ink were combined with wash in the boat study below. In this sketch, more attention has been devoted to the composition of the separate elements into an integrated design. A comparison of the two sketches will clarify the difference between these two methods.

MONTE ALBAN

DRY DOCK

Forgotten Corner

This is another frankly descriptive sketch that depends on its story-telling content for interest. Generally I discount this element in a picture, preferring to let the intrinsic art qualities—the plastic content, design, tonal arrangement, and handling of the medium—be the real story. I dis-

"Monte Alban", the wash and pen drawing at the top of page 46, was made at the Mayan ruins near Monte Alban in Oaxaca, Mexico. Fine dotted lines, broad bamboo pen strokes, strong areas of black washes help to build up a full tonal range for contrast and impact. The wet-in-wet technique was used in places; a few final touches of opaque white were used discreetly to outline a passage or break up a monotonous area.

Dispersions of ink on very wet paper were used to suggest mud and pebble textures in the foreground of "Dry Dock", reproduced at the bottom of page 46. Fine pen lines were drawn in over broad brush work when wash areas were dry.

like paintings that must have a peg to hang on, whether it be a clever title or some other device.

"Forgotten Corner" has some of this weakness about it, but the subject, aside from its story-telling quality, provided a fine exercise in the use of wash. Everything is recorded meticulously, from the price of gas when the final gallon was sold, to the rusting tin cup dangling from the water pump. Broken window panes, a thermometer on the faded wall, a cat prowling about the deserted store—all of these, set in a weed-shrouded landscape evoke an overwhelming feeling of desolation and some nostalgia for the almost forgotten glory of the old country store.

Although the washes appear fresh, they have been worked over and modeled carefully. Lights were saved and scratched out with sandpaper and razor blade. The weeds were touched in with a sharp point. A precise drawing was made in pencil before the washes were applied with a large sable brush. A small pointed sable was used for detail drawing.

This study was used for a full-color painting made later in the studio. The original was completed in two hours on location.

Flowers

For the floral study at left, brush and quill pen were used on a damp hot-press (smooth surface) Strathmore paper. A rapid impression such as this should be done directly with the brush, without preliminary pencil delineation of the forms. No attempt was made to render accurate botanical detail. The purpose of this type of study is to capture some of the variety of design forms in an over-all unity, filling the page with a decorative line and mass. The elongated vertical shape of the paper accents the shape and composition of the arrangement, adding to its interest.

The brush drawing at right was made in sepia with watercolor on dry paper. Here the flower forms were carefully observed and meticulously drawn, with more attention devoted to individual flower blossoms than in the sketch above. Such drawings sacrifice sparkle and freedom of execution, but are a valuable source of study. Both drawings were done on full sheets of watercolor paper.

Winter Fields

A combination technique was used in the painting reproduced above. First the paper was dampened; over this a hard-rubber roller was used to make a few diagonal washes. The sky area was drawn with a few broad, flat strokes of a gray conté chalk. While the paper was still damp, a pen was used to draw in the fine lines of the branches in the foreground; some splatter and dots were added at the same time. A broad brush was employed for the dark areas of the farm buildings after the paper had dried. A touch of the razor blade etched out the few white accents. The drawing was sprayed lightly with a fixative to fix the pastel strokes before framing.

A SUGGESTED SHORT COURSE OF STUDY

Although you may not care to be bothered by such things as course outlines or timetables, you may find that some kind of study program will help you to make faster progress in wash drawing than haphazard trial and vague experiment will allow.

The sessions of study indicated here will prevent repetition and wasted time. If you are just beginning to do wash drawings, and follow the series of techniques and exercises listed below, you will be gratified with the improvement appearing in your work after a few months of concentrated effort.

1. Materials

A session devoted exclusively to investigating materials and their characteristics. Make comparisons of different blacks: inks, watercolors, sumi sticks. Try them in terms of density, diluting strength. Compare the lines and strokes of bamboo sticks, writing pens, brushes. Study the texture and absorbency of an assortment of papers. Experiment with rubber cement, masking, sponges. Complete familiarity with the materials of wash drawing is essential preparation for the study to come.

2. The Simple and Gradated Wash

This is a basic exercise on which much time should be spent. Try painting a flat, even gray wash, flowing the wash on evenly from side to side, not scrubbing it on. Begin at the top of a large page and *flow* the wash with a large brush, first down the page, then from side to side. Mix a quantity of medium gray wash first. Then gradate the wash, gradually adding black pigment. Paint a chart of ten evenly spaced tones from white to black, creating a step-ladder of tone. Try a wash on top of a wash, after the first is dry. Try a wash on wet paper. Try making washes with flat and pointed brushes.

3. Line Patterns

Compose a chart of line patterns, as shown on page 14. Invent your own kind of textures, using pointed brushes and broad flat sable. Cut down old bristle brushes and use them for stipple textures. Try simple line designs using a bamboo stick over wash. Experiment with line designs on wet paper.

4. Linear Drawing

Devote a number of hours to drawing in outline from objects, using pen and brush. Use this exercise to develop control of eye and hand. Try free scribble lines around forms; combine line silhouette with interior lines around and through objects. These are merely practice scales which you can forget when you begin to make music.

5. Composing a Subject

Select material for rendering in limited tones—three or four grays. Organize the spotting of blacks, the spacing of white areas. Use a few linear textures and choose a large, easy subject for your first drawing; a house, a barn, a hill, a road.

6. Further Techniques

Try dry brush, sponge, stencil, masking. Consult the illustrations in this book and attempt similar subjects to develop technical dexterity. Try varieties of razor-blade scratching and picking out of lights on wet and dry papers.

7. The Wet-In-Wet Technique

Prepare a page of trial experiments. Drop in ink lines, brush strokes; try the flicked-brush and spatter techniques. Only practice can teach you how much ink to pick up in the brush, and how much water, and how damp the paper must be to make an ink line run and disperse.

8. Further Drawing Problems

Sketch out-of-doors with directed study. One day draw trees; another, houses. Read Norton's *"Perspective Made Easy,"* or Ernest Watson's *"Creative Perspective."* Collect sketchbook material for development in the studio. Make studies from the figure in line and wash.

9. Semi-Abstract Renderings

Try imaginative and non-figurative paintings using combined techniques. Invent shapes and designs which do not depend upon literal fact or visual reference. Experiment with tones, textures and washes in a free "doodle" style to loosen your approach.

10. Study of Early Classical Styles

Visit the library and study the Chinese and Japanese traditions, the early masters of drawing in wash. Search out the drawings of Turner, Girtin and the English watercolorists of the 19th century. Try painting a tree in the classic style. Study the wash drawings of Cézanne. Visit a contemporary exhibition to observe the latest techniques and creative tendencies.

11. Matting and Framing

Examine your work and select a few of the best things you have done. Dress them up in mats. Spend an hour being your own critic, determining how the work could be improved.

12. Enjoy Yourself!

Treat yourself to the finest sketchbook available, some sheets of expensive watercolor stock, a new sable brush and a paint box—but only if you have worked hard on the preceding lessons and deserve them.

Steal away to a quiet spot that you have always wanted to paint. Today may be the day. With luck and a lot of hard work behind you, it *may* happen! That marvelous sketch where everything goes right, where the accidents fall into the right places, the lines sing, and the washes glow, is waiting to be done and now may be the time. When this *does* happen—you'll know!

WARRIOR
John Baldwin

"Warrior" is one of the many sketches made by John Baldwin as preliminary studies for welded sculpture. Painted rapidly on wet paper, it is a strong design, interesting in the use of open forms suggestive of dimension and space.

MUSIC
Joe Lasker

"Music" was executed in ink washes on thin tissue paper. This is a beautifully conceived direct brush drawing. Notice the trial sketches of the children's heads, and the use of rich black areas.

54

THE BUTTERFLIES
Leonard Brooks

"Butterflies" was drawn with brush and pen on rough, wet watercolor paper. Fine lines were added with a pen after the paper had dried.

SPRING FETE
Dan Lutz

In "Spring Fète", the artist used wash and line, with some opaque touches, to develop the forms of figures and trees into a lively composition. Notice the consistently free execution, the absence of superfluous detail.

HORSES
John Young

The original drawing of "Horses" was painted in ink on a linen canvas surface. Free, flowing lines fill the picture with rhythmic vitality.

55

WINTER ROOT
Fred Samuelson

"Winter Root" exploits many of the textural qualities which are demonstrated in this book, including spottings, wet-in-wet, scrapings and "controlled accidents." This is a fine example of inventive picture-making in the medium of wash drawing.

THE PREDATORS
José Chávez Morado

"The Predators" is an expressive drawing by José Chávez Morado, the Mexican painter-muralist. Here the wash technique serves the artist well in establishing a haunting dark mood as the background for a white pigeon.

ON THE BRIDGE
Robert Maxwell

"On the Bridge" is a lively, free drawing executed with brush and pen. The composition is developed with black silhouetted brush-strokes and a strong use of spotting with white and black.

FIGURE
James Pinto

In "Figure", a fluid line drawn on dampened paper traces exciting patterns over the white area of the figure, creating an effective linear design.

BEGGAR
Louis Ribak

This drawing demonstrates a most skillful handling of line and wash by a fine painter. Notice particularly the free pen line, with broad washes of shadow superimposed to establish the monumental solidity of the subject.

BIBLIOGRAPHY OF USEFUL BOOKS

ARTISTS ON ART
 Goldwater and Treves
 Pantheon Books

CÉZANNE DRAWINGS
 Alfred Neumeyer
 Thomas Yoseloff

HOW TO USE CREATIVE PERSPECTIVE
 Ernest Watson
 Reinhold

ENJOYING MODERN ART
 Sarah Newmeyer
 Reinhold

FIGURE DRAWING COMES TO LIFE
 Albert, Calvin and Seckler, Dorothy
 Reinhold

JAPANESE INK-PAINTING
 Ryukyu Saito
 Tuttle

ON THE LAWS OF JAPANESE PAINTING
 Henry P. Bowie
 Dover Books

PAINTING TREES AND LANDSCAPES
IN WATERCOLOR
 Ted Kautzky
 Reinhold

THE CHANGING FORMS OF ART
 Patrick Heron
 Noonday Press, Inc.

THE ENDURING ART OF JAPAN
 Langdon Warner
 Grove Press

THE HOKUSAI SKETCHBOOK
 James Michener
 Tuttle

THE LANDSCAPE PAINTING OF CHINA AND JAPAN
 Hugo Munsterberg
 Tuttle

THE NATURAL WAY TO DRAW
 Kimon Nicolaides
 Houghton & Mifflin

THE PAINTER'S EYE
 Maurice Grosser
 A Mentor Book

THE TAO OF PAINTING
 Bollingen Series XLIX

THE WAY OF CHINESE PAINTING
 Mai-mai Sze
 Modern Library Paperbook

TREATISE ON LANDSCAPE PAINTING
 Andre Lhote
 Zwemmer, London

WATERCOLOR—A CHALLENGE
 Leonard Brooks
 Reinhold

WATER-COLOUR, A TRULY ENGLISH ART
 Percy V. Bradshaw
 The Studio Publications